Elegy

Raphaela Willington

POEMS

SBN 978-1-936373-32-1

© 2012 The Judy Willington Trust.

All rights reserved. No part of this publication may be reproduced or transmitted in any form or by any means, electronic or mechanical, without permission in writing from the publisher. Requests for permission to make copies of any part of this work should be e-mailed to info @ unboundcontent.com.

Published in the United States by
Unbound Content, LLC, Englewood, NJ.
All drawings by Raphaela Willington
© The Judy Willington Trust.
Cover art by Raphaela Willington
© The Judy Willington Trust.
Author photos and Foreword by John Briggs
© John Briggs.

Elegy
First edition 2012

Contents

Foreword	9
Sometimes You Wake	20
Three Large Icicles	21
Bury Me	22
Prayer's Shadow	23
Roses in Winter	24
I Bury the Paperwhites	25
The Jungle of Memory-Entangled Vines	26
This Day	28
Close to Death	29
Outside in Still Deep Snow	30
The Lyric Sun	31
Like an Animal	32
Hawk's Shadow	33
My Dreams Have Become Trees	34
Shades of Winter	36
Midwinter	37
As the Crows Fly	38
Winter Trees	39
Cold Shades	40
Spring Fear	41
For What Is Over and Gone	42
Missing Snow	43

Endgame	44
Impossibly Alive	46
Sitting in Sun	47
No Place to Go	48
The Deer and I	49
Nor'easter	50
Human Heart	51
Bride	52
Mourning Doves	53
Wedding	54
Dogwoods	55
Memory	56
To a Mangled Squirrel	57
Revelation	58
Wrensong	59
A Glorious Summer's Day	60
Neighborhood Picnic	61
Summering	62
Woodchuck	63
Air Tragedy	64
Picking Peas on Earth	65
In the Garden	68
Waking in Paradise	70
Monday Morning, August	71
An Old Maple	72
Gladioli, Equinox '99	73

Elegy to Mother and Dad	74
Mid-day	75
Growing Seasons	76
Fifth Anniversary	77
End of September	78
Country Room	80
What's Wrong with Dying	81
Suburban Elegy	83
In Memory of Mom and Dad	85
Unmaking the Bed	86
On Our Parents' Death	87
An Epitaph for Ashes	88
Harvest 1996	89
Cadence	91
Acorns	93
Nearwinter Sun Is Rising	94
Each Shape	95
Exceptions	96
After Thanksgiving	97
Winter Arrives	98
The Paperweight	99
Arcadian Gardens	100
Poem to Death, Winter Solstice	101

Foreword

Raphaela Willington died on January 6, 2004, of ovarian cancer. Death became her muse in her last years. But her dark inspiration arose not only in response to her cancer. I remember one night at 2 a.m. in September 1997, two years after she'd received her grim prognosis and suffered through many months of an aggressive chemotherapy that made her feel she was near to death, or "worse than death," I was awakened by a phone call. She was telephoning from her parents' home in Briarcliff, New York. "John, don't freak out," her first concern for my reaction. She said a state trooper had come to the door to inform her that both her parents had just been killed in an horrific car crash on their way home from visiting her sister, Karen, and Karen's family in Boston. I remember vividly that the tone in my friend's voice conveyed a calm that awakened me to how much she had become an intimate with death and would accommodate these deaths, too.

An important part of how she accomplished that accommodation is manifest in these poems. Philosopher Martin Heidegger observed that "death is capable of the greatest lighting up of *being* and its truth." Death is never far from most artists' minds, which means that *being* in its intensity is also never far. After I suggested to my friend that she make a collection of her poems about death, it was not surprising to me that some of those she chose showed dates of composition before she had learned of her cancer. Nevertheless, the poems in this collection were selected, revised, sequenced, and sharpened by the elegiac perceptions that accompanied what she jokingly referred to as "my crash course in dying."

My old friend Raphaela lived an obscure and largely quiet life. In an age of public lives she was a private person. Her relationship with her parents — both of them high strung and psychologically conflicted individuals — had been difficult for her growing up and, later, difficult for her as a young woman and as a married woman. In the last 15 years of her life, following her divorce, she had made a very conscious and concerted effort to repair her "family of origin" relationships. She and her mother gardened together. Her father came to appreciate her as a calming, even therapeutic, influence. It is fair to say that in the year or two before her parents died, the three of them had become friends. Perhaps that doesn't sound like much of an accomplishment, but to someone like myself who had known the family for years from outside, it seemed remarkable.

I always knew her as Judy. That was the name she had when I first met her in fourth grade. We were lifelong friends. She was the sister I never had (she had a younger sister and I a younger brother). During some periods we lost touch with each other. In high school she was our class poet and we other aspiring writers much admired and envied her incisive and preternaturally mature style; her ability to translate complex emotional states into words. In high school and long afterward, with some exceptions, she made bad choices with men.

In her 20s she married a brilliant and thwarted writer with a dominating personality, and throughout their marriage her own writing stayed in the background. But she kept persistently at it. She never made much effort to seek publication or even show her poems to friends, though she always worked at them with professional and uncompromising care. In that way she was like a poet she much admired, Emily Dickinson. She left behind over 300 carefully crafted poems. She was a child of the 60s and lived for a time the bohemian life of her generation. She never had children, which she regretted. Later, she studied Tibetan Buddhism. She did odd jobs of editing. She was an accomplished and published astrologer, though she was tolerant and sympathetic to my skepticism of the occult practice, which I had dabbled in myself. We both had an interest in the philosopher-mystic Jiddu Krishnamurti and so all of her beliefs — reincarnation, astrology, the *I Ching* — included a level of skepticism which we discussed at great length. I always admired the fact that her beliefs in Buddhism or the occult never served as a protection from the unknown and the uncertainty to which she gave herself with great courage.

1970s

Beyond her poetry, her deepest belief was in her garden — especially her vegetable garden — as it changed from year to year. I see her as someone who never found a place in the world and in the end seemed satisfied to have no place. After her parents died she kept their house just as it was, with few traces of her own. When she died she was cremated and at her request there was no funeral or memorial marker, no notification even, except to a few close friends. Years ago she had taken the name Judy Willington to replace her original Judy Jacobs, I think because it gave her a certain aesthetic distance on herself. She had her name changed officially by a rabbi after she got sick. Her parents witnessed. Raphaela was her chosen first name for her writing, and made the aesthetic distance more complete. It was her pen name for her life more than for her writing. But that meant when we spread her ashes in the garden we couldn't be sure who we were burying.

Shortly after we scattered her ashes we had to sell her parents' house for the estate. The garden with her in it became a building lot for another structure. I know she wanted simply to pass away without fanfare.

A culture plumped with its belief in self-importance and fixated on amassing accomplishment might judge that Raphaela didn't "do" much with her life. She sometimes thought that might be the case and felt guilty about it. But what she didn't accomplish—children, a career, a public life—provided a hidden benefit. The aesthetic distance she achieved through the way she lived her life gives her poems, in my estimation, an exquisite stillness and nobility. As a result they provide a unique kind of solace in their contemplation of our common destiny.

I encouraged her to collect the poems and arrange them as she wanted, and this became a project which she worked at steadily, as energy permitted, during her last year and a half. Many of the scenes described in the poems take place at her parents' home in Westchester County where she often stayed, making her garden there and observing the activities of the surrounding woods. These supplied the terms for her metaphors. All of the drawings interspersed in the poems are hers, most from a period in New York City when she took botanical drawing classes. She liked the idea of including the drawings in the collection and chose which ones I should use.

    Rereading the poems, I find myself immersed in my friend's world. The garden she tended. The window out of which she and Javier, her companion of some 20 years, watched the birds. The brooding snowscape of winter. The staggering profusion of blossoms from her flowerbeds in spring. I remember the rooms I passed through in the several years I visited her at her parents' home. The light through the tall curtained windows in the cavernous living room strewn with her mother's abstract marble sculptures. I remember the presence of her awareness which seemed everywhere in that place. Others reading her poems will construct their own place and awareness out of the details she selected.

    Eleven days after the events of 9/11/2001, in nearby New York City, Raphaela's Buddhist colleague Susan visited her in Ossining and recalls moments similar to many I spent with my old friend. Susan told me, "We sat in the breakfast room and watched all the birds feeding just outside. There were so many—titmice, chickadees, cardinals, blackbirds, doves, and others. I even saw a flicker. Just past the tree from which the bird feeders hung was a large bush fully in bloom, and many butterflies—monarchs and a few small white ones too—were feeding on its blossoms. As we ate lunch, a faun, half grown but still wearing his spots, came by and nibbled at the lower branches of one of the small trees near the house. We talked until I was hoarse. It was a wonderful visit, one of those rare times out of time — and for a little while we thought of something other than the past week's tragedies."

In the winter of 2003 I called her from a pay phone while I was on a trip to Death Valley. I naturally cajoled her about the name of the place where I was as a parallel to the place where she was. We had long since established that the important thing was not to pussyfoot around the mortality issue, but to confront it directly. She appreciated that I was willing to do that, though for me it wasn't as easy as I wanted her to think.

That time was one of several periods when we weren't sure she would make it much longer. She had a serious intestinal obstruction and I thought we might lose her before I returned from California. Doctors were urging her to undergo a surgery that could prolong her life, but she felt ambivalent about it. During the call she reported a dream. "I'm a fish and I think I'm cleaned, sliced and boned and ready for the frying pan. I should be hearing the sizzling, instead I hear them say they want to throw me back into the water to swim around and be nibbled by the big fish trying to take a bite out of me."

Later in the month, after I returned from my trip, I made a journal entry: "Taking her driving to get chocolate, one of the few things she can eat with any pleasure, her gut bloated with the tumor, she talked about not having children as a risk factor for ovarian cancer. We laughed at my suggestion that she was now pregnant with death. But aside from the bloating, which was hidden under loose clothes, she looked beautiful, a handsome 58-year-old woman, her face thin and sensual. We talked about the sometimes sickening certainty of 'religious' people. She declared that despite the Buddhism she was not a religious person. It was clear that before her lay not certainty but a bottomless puzzlement which she regarded with an equanimity I could only admire. In the coffee shop, watching a young child in an orange jumpsuit with a glowing face like a tiny Buddhist monk, she said, 'To have to go through all that again. It starts with such natural wonder and joy and then gets lost in all this crap.'"

Later she decided to have the surgery which might prolong her life for a few months, too many of which she knew would be taken up with recovery from the operation. In her dark humor, she suggested that her body parts might be saved for love poems and that she should make a collage of her tumor. She wondered if she would fart in the face of the surgeon when he "turned my rectum upside down." Lying in her bed at White Plains Hospital after the surgery she did a riff on the tubes arcing out of her and what the color of her internal liquids revealed about her life and the world. It was spontaneous and hilarious. I told her it would have made a great stand-up comic monologue. "I've always wanted to be a stand-up comic," she said, "But if I stood up in front of a whole bunch of people, I'd have to pee."

In November of 2003, a month from the end, I made a dated note of a phone call: "Today she spoke of an immense sadness. She didn't want to see me, anybody, because the engagement would be too overwhelming, the sense of the past and the future. Physical presence puts her back into the life she is leaving." Four days later she observed on the phone, "Everyone is given a trick-or-treat bag with certain candies and they spend their lives trying to get the candies other people have."

In her last months alive—late summer and harvest time—she sometimes asked to be moved to a chair by the window. The fast-metabolizing cancer made her hot and she wanted the window open to feel the air. Javier had done the vegetable garden for her that last summer. She had no energy to do it, but she was grateful that the garden was out there growing.

Even as she became what Yeats called "a rag upon a stick" she retained her biting humor. Javier, advised by the hospice personnel, whispered to her in her drugged and fetal state that it was "okay to go." She unexpectedly opened one eye and flashed a sly smile. "You want to go with me," she whispered back. We all had a good laugh.

The last few days were appropriately bizarre. Judy drifted in and out, sometimes seeing Bosch-like figures popping out and floating across the bookshelves and wall. Javier whispered on the phone to Karen about final arrangements, the nurse knitted in the corner beside the dark television screen. In the midst of this, my own anxiety drove me to feel an urgency to pay bills and I rushed in to get Judy's signature. She refused, looking cross-eyed at what she said was a "hinnie" hallucination lurking in the cupboard. It was pointless, she said, the bills would all roll over to the estate anyway "after I'm kaput." The word "kaput" and the detached way she said it have echoed with me through the years.

At the end of a life what remains? In fact, nothing remains, of course. Time eventually dissolves everything. Raphaela's poems present the strangely joyous flavors of that brooding nothingness that makes our life so full.

At one point as we were working on this collection, I asked her to write up a brief biography of herself and then felt dissatisfied with her result: "Raphaela Willington lived, worked, and wrote in New York City and Westchester County, New York. She was fond of gardening in her later years." I have since come to see that the biography beautifully and succinctly expressed her life.

When I told her that I wanted to write a foreword to the collection, she said she wanted to see it. I think she was curious to read what I could possibly say about her. I said I didn't know if I had enough time to write it down before the end. (In fact, for emotional reasons I couldn't write it at all for six years.) She laughed and said time was an issue for her, too. To illustrate she pulled a poem out of a drawer and said that she had wanted it in the collection but what with dealing with the disease and choosing and arranging the other poems, she didn't have enough time to revise the piece. "Besides, it takes me three years to revise a poem." She stopped and smiled. "So I guess I'll have to take it with me." The line was intended to make

Early spring 2003, shortly after surgery to remove an intestinal blockage, her garden behind her.

me laugh, and I did. She persisted, "You could tape it to my chest when they put me in the box to cremate me." I said if I did that, then I could use her as an ultimate example for my students of commitment to the revision process. Later, discussing the design of the book, she proposed in jest that I should do the cover in the form of a tombstone. As much as anything, she was gently chafing me for pushing her to make such a collection because she worried that its subject was morbid. I'm happy to say that the poems she chose and arranged prove that her fear was unfounded.

John Briggs

January 2, 1994

Sometimes You Wake

Sometimes you wake
into silence

Slowly your ears adjust
to birds creating a ruckus
or simply pronouncing morning's joyful name

Vibrant with the state of not waiting,
you observe the signs and penetrations
into or out of the silence:
a firtree's shadow,
the curled leaves of the rhododendron,
prints on the snowslope of an unimaginable animal

January 5, 2003

Three Large Icicles

*On receiving John's postcard
from Death Valley*

Day by day,
Death claims me
Trees branch me to the sky

There is more dark at my back
and a distinctness things have
when I look at them

Three large icicles pend from the eaves,
a hill of trees at their back
like the dark at mine

A distant shadow,
you close in on me

slow and hinder my escape
It seems you do it for my sake,
as one who remembers

The world — thy world and mine —
freezes leaves together

January 8, 1994

Bury Me

Bury me beneath snow
When my bones show
in spring take pity
on their homelessness

Grind them into calcium
beat upon a drum with them
anything but don't ignore
their splintered sense

Look with care
on these remains!
If one or more
are out of place
wait until you've figured out

exactly how they fit
This is now possible —
no flesh and blood conceal...

I think no better ending
might be made
than lying strewn
upon the ground
like willow fronds

January 12, 1994

Prayer's Shadow

All prayers spoken at Time's Origin
were sufficient.
Pray them once —
a prayer's shadow is an endless echo.

Some wonder if any Heart were present,
when images of cardinal and jay crisscrossed
from hemlock to hemlock
the first time,
whether an archetypal couple
swayed wild new bodies in other prayer.

Some Heart responds or will
to all questioning —
when the last demon is freed from hell,
the last footprint replaced by flame,
when flame too dissolves
into the heat of flame alone.
And, then, the echo of a final utterance
floating out over what used to be night.

January 14, 1993

Roses in Winter

Clipped from a downed limb
spruce branches warm rose roots

Last leaves, late growth
Crumpled stalks, snowbrushed
The railroad tie embankment
you built for them

Day, snow intensified
Whitened trees
All these riverwaters
and tall tall wooded places

This sunless time
sunsetless time
snowdusted
This sunsetless time
Trainwhistle
vaguely registered

When the magic cape is lifted
the magician is beneath,
like a black squirrel
at the feet of the pines

January 16, 1998

I Bury the Paperwhites

I bury the paperwhites,
the narcissus,
as you did, Mother
I bury one; I bury two;
I bury you, again

Before their planting they had grown
into near stems
reaching for light,
their dark skins
in contrast with your pale

I barely breathe
since September
How, why should I
when you no longer do
It is as if
these blooms

will breathe for us
Deep, pungent,
white as Death's
unreachableness

January 17, 2000

The Jungle of Memory-Entangled Vines

You leave a legacy of love among
the now poignant trappings of your lives,
the shrubs and the furniture,
the paintings and the garden things.

Words spoken to and about you over the years
resound as counterpoint
to the officer's announcement of the accident.

A stillness arises, as if from your bones —
wherever they may be — on their shattered way
to eternity, draped in rags of what you had been
     wearing.

Since then, the calm has come and gone,
come and gone. It is what I anticipate
day after mendicant day, and it follows
the crash into my heart, my bittersweet voicing of
     your names.

In this jungle of memory-entangled vines,
in response to my call,
in lieu of the stillness, yesterday

you reached me by telephone,
a wrong number.
Darling, it said, this is Mother.
And her husband added his hello,
as Dad used to.

January 18, 1994

This Day

This day is in and of itself a poem
that sorrows and pities cannot dull
I have lived inside it once before
when words mapped woods like dappled deer
and vision trailed them

The sun is today a citadel
falling falling
yet standing
And shadows beneath trees
secret apses known to none save priests
and priestesses of Snow

In ages past and yet to come
each speck of rainbowed frost
each icicle like a tree reversed
roots curled up over roof and sills
each breathing branch beneath

its crest of Snow
echoed and will echo
as with silver trumpets
what has been this day

To dedicate to Love is not enough
For what beloved dares give half as much

January 24, 1994

Close to Death

Living close to death,
the beauty of snow on trees
melts into caesura
like no other.
As if someone you loved left.
Fears realized.
Heart broken.
Meaningless omens willed, now,
to the superstitions
of the world around you.
What used to send tremors
through your body
becomes a simple fact of living,
like breathing.
How unlike the years of dreaming!

As cold, white clumps tumble off branches
to the ground below,
a memory returns — sleek,
evoking desire, some spark perhaps
of long iced-over passion.
It seems wrong, with death
so prominent in the landscape.
Like children at a grownup party,
this intuition of Spring,
the kiss of Life
that wakes the Dead of Winter.

January 24, 1994

Outside in Still Deep Snow

Outside in still deep snow
what seems a blot
becomes a bird
lying in state
under the yew

Ravages that took time
seem suddenly disastrous — final
graybrown stiff as pain

Never good luck
death whirls life into disarray

As day progresses
the image reverberates
sporadically distracting...

Dead bird, true icon of time
like Wind in Trees
Mind of Nights to come
Days Whose Storms Do End

January 29, 1993

The Lyric Sun

The lyric sun will never melt us,
shortlived like snow,
part myth like the Pleiades
part effervescent truth

The sound of ravencalls
the play of nervous squirrels
are nourishment,
oxygen for dying persons

As if in anticipation,
the moon nightly nurses our bodiless dreams

Each morning
waking frames a door
and breathing a hallway
Songs condense intrinsic dark
singing themselves voiceless
among such light

January 29, 1996

Like an Animal

Like an animal
I do not believe
the furry corpse before my eyes
matted hair and stiffened flesh

Like an animal
I root through everything
searching with ancestral eyes
to find the trail
that leads away from death

January 29, 2000

Hawk's Shadow

Is that the dead I hear singing
about the deer, as the shadow
of a hawk scrapes the snow?
Bluegray striping white—
phantom trunk and branch stretch out below.

The frigid winter sun lives on
almost nothing at this time.
Its cold reflections feed the does
and bucks and seem to fatten them.

Squirrels gather,
eating spill-off from the feeder.
Outlines of dead and dying trees
rise up perpendicular
from the hill beyond the house.
Where do they point or lead?

Let us pretend
we are a part of one another's lives again,
together, over dinner.

January 31, 1994

My Dreams Have Become Trees

My Dreams have become Trees
yet not as I had pictured them
Towering pines near lakes
have been replaced
by landscaped hedges —
laurel, azalea, hemlock, yew
Surrounding woods have blessed
the lawn with shadows
altering Winter's shape, dimensions,
sometimes speed
when arctic winds exhale

How am I to wake in future
when these leaves and stalks and needles
drop into the final Wintering
Must I sleep forever then
dreaming of a coming eon
Drafting bark and branch and stem
upon the quiet table of my mind
Grafting prints from fossiled trunks
onto the emptiest times

when those remaining in the Shell —
jay, fattest stealer of them all,
and squirrels who treat the willow
well, in gratitude for sheltering arms

and wandering humans whose Millenium
has lasted since Edenic calm—
arise to enter into tryst
with None
and All
and Paradigm

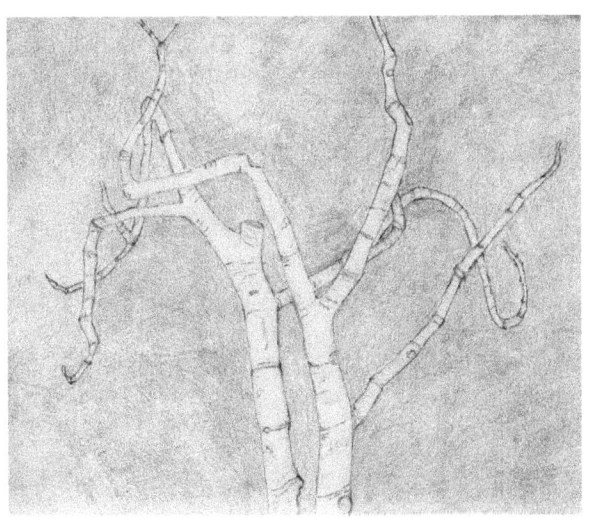

January 1997

Shades of Winter

For Betty Freudenheim and Joan Rosenblatt

Two women I did not know well are dead;
tonight they wander in snow.

If I ask them in,
what will we talk about?

How steadily falling snow
creates the illusion
of petering out?

February 4, 1993

Midwinter

Under a lunar stare,
veiny branchtips sift incoming night.
Deer dance
around what they cannot eat.

Earth seems to fly from sun,
and I to dream.
The cricket wintering in our house
hardly dances at all.

February 26, 1993

As the Crows Fly

I wonder
can I interpret the language
of crows
as they fly diagonally
across the lawn
into trees
Beyond sight
their cries resound

Returning diagonally
in the direction
from which they came
they float
silent as snow

This afternoon in winter
as in summer
not one tip of evergreen sways
not one leafless twig
As inner crows illuminate our minds
with acts of deathless love

February 1993

Winter Trees

Winter trees
on earthy mounds
like hillocks of graves
North or darker, colder side,
a living shade

Inspiration quavers below zero
Thoughts like soundless shrieks
neighborhood crows cannot outscreech
The frozen soul stays dormant
and renunciative

February 1994

Cold Shades

Morning puts night under cover
Blinds clicked into position
Outside lights off, still bright enough
for pale detection

of how love once responded
filling the day after
memory aromatic, wafting
into the next round of loving

Now-tired eyes scout
the scent of possibility
guessing from remarks
wondering at implications

With all this snow
deer have fled
squirrels forego the feeder
and birds are few

Drifts pile up nearly to windows
as friends fill the day with chatter
Words replace hands

There is a fear of walking outside in such cold
a fear the Heart will freeze
and fix among unmelting eternals
forever

February 12, 1998

Spring Fear

I am afraid of spring now you are gone,
Mother.
That your favorite blossoming trees
will carry you away
from my haven, memory.
The reality of them,
expressing the season,
may overwhelm my senses
and I shall fall deeper
into that moment of the past
when you left,
when my regretful love wandered,
interred,
when we were one loss.

March 18, 1997

For What Is Over and Gone

The cardinal observes
in his quick, quiet way
the circle of lawn and trees,
the unplanted garden.

He is the perfect foil
for the colorless remainder of winter,
except for a sprig of leaves
on the Japanese red maple.

In one week, or two,
the first hyacinths,
then daffodils,
will pierce up through earth.

In spring,
one cannot imagine
never having loved.

March 29, 1993

Missing Snow

This morning
most snow was missing
after last night's rain.
Only banks remain
where the snowplow left them.

Having survived winter,
the earth lies tamed
in time for Spring's excitation.

Here,
not just anywhere
near another Star.

March 24, 2000

Endgame

Spring brings fresh heat.
Nothing shows itself easily.
Foliage on tulips-to-be is scattered and occasional,
the lawn, drought-brown and clumpy.
The landscaper's son, who has taken over the
        business,
puts off early seeding that needs to be done.
One afternoon he arrives unannounced with his wife
        and new baby.
The boy, unmoving, sleeps through our conversation.

So far this year, the garden helper has not appeared.
Perennials need unmulching, roses pruning, and
the grasses shearing to the ground.
To get something done, we hang birdhouse gourds
        on branches of trees,
attracting some wrens and a multitude of squirrels.
Seed catalogues clothe the dining room table,
the latest I have got to them in years.

Since the equinox, and after a long dry spell,
my dreams have started up again.
I dream of the grail king;
he seems a clue to this unprecedented spring.
An ailing king, a tired property.
As with so many endings, a sense of sorrow
        winds its threads

from room to room to shrub to tree.

I follow its trail into the woods surrounding
      the house and lawn
and discover the skull of a young buck,
      still antlered,
flesh not fully disappeared from bone.
One ear remains intact, as if listening, I imagine,
for the sound of the voice of my father calling us,
      mother and me,
in from the dusk of the garden
      at the end of a long day.

March 31, 1993

Impossibly Alive

Life dreamt
and waked to the rhythm of
wide awake bird
whose call
even at dusk
plunges through dark

The bird and his song
accompany us

Suddenly geese
beloved and irreversible
against blue night

April 4, 1994

Sitting in Sun

Sitting in sun
awaiting the right moon for sowing
spring
welcomed simply for its being
revels in naturalness
snowmoldy grass
winterburned trees
immense crows
(patterned like notes on a staff
of highest branches only)

All seem storytelling
who we were together
new-faced now from lifetimes lived apart
millenia-dimmed visions
pushing up into spring
into a love so hoped for

April 18, 2001

No Place to Go

Lost in the wilderness
of my parents' house,
my illness,
I inherit:
the bounce of a branch of hemlock,
your embrace

April 8, 1995

The Deer and I

We face off
They, in woods near the house
I, on the drive

They do not run,
nor I

Together we stare
through the gray veil of day
at a memory, a mother

who left her fawns
struggling to survive

A buck cavorts
across the lawn
and shoos a crow away

April 13, 1997

Nor'easter

Tonight the sun set on my heart.
And stars that clarity of night allows
were more than I could bear to know were there.

The day was filled with crows and daffodils.
Trees uprooted from the storm
lay across the path
like lines of omen on a palm.
Where it was sawed, the dogwood bled incessantly.
Piles of chips were yesterday's locust and apple trees.

Gold forsythia, April diadem.
Blossoms from the weeping cherry,
jewels scattered by the lords of wind.

April 14, 1996

Human Heart

I am like a deer in the forest
or a bird
The crack of a branch underfoot—
I leap, or fly

Then,
resisting my own heart,
I run with the herd,
flock in formation
Wake in the morning, passionless

Only Your love can sustain
my hoof or wing
exultant above dead winter grass,
bronze my flight
upon Heaven's mantelpiece

April 17, 1998

Bride

I am the bride of sweet alyssum,
and daffodils,
and my parents' death.

Trying to name the tagless shrubs,
dialing to tell the news
of their death.

Under crisp, full moons
encircling radiant suns,
the as-yet-unborn
accompanying them.
Among treetop and trellis,
I cannot yet divorce from
the Life of their lives.
I have not the momentum.

Waking each morning,
I blush at returning
to weeding and sowing.

April 22, 2000

Mourning Doves

I am the mourning doves.
Among the ricocheting birds of spring
and their ricochet of sudden song,
I fly and flee and start to remember
the wilder instincts of the season.

I am, particularly, the mateless dove,
since both of you are gone.

Snowdrops have bloomed.
Narcissi and forsythia unwrap in shades
      of yellow,
lilacs ready to follow.
Tulips from past years mingle with last fall's.

I wing out onto the waiting branch
that may or may not hold me.

April 23, 1998

Wedding

Pray for the flowering trees.
Murmur to pink dogwood.
Kneel beneath the gently gnarled apple.

As copper bells chime in rainsoaked wind,
trees bloom for a fraction of a season.

Briefly in color, briefly alive.
Like the self,
an ecstatic, momentary, grieving bride.

April 2002

Dogwoods

This year the dogwoods are crisp,
says Don, who prunes trees and shrubs
for us
This year, the petals shine at dusk
like the snow
that did not fall last winter

I lay among petals and soon to be
      leafed-out branches
The birdhouse you built was in part, I knew,
a response to what life had become

I lay waiting on what had been mother's bed,
wondering when the wrens would come
to wake me every morning
with their song

New Moon, May 1993

Memory

For Helen

I am so old
I have lost all sense of time
of the passing of time

Wandering
among unmanageable thoughts —
once passions —
retracing prints of meaning
Sleepless, corrupt, undainty
as the lunar surface

Sedated only by the rhythm
of a beating heart
pounding at the fringes of universes
among dancing beacons
once thought to be stars

June 18, 1995

To a Mangled Squirrel
(an offering of philosophy)

We are told
each death is our own
The shattered squirrel
tells me

I take spade to the road
where, maggot-ridden, halved,
and disembowelled,
my other self lies
waiting to be joined
to earth
to death without belief
in prayer, image,
or eternity

June 1993

Revelation

When my world ends
let stick and leaf and stream
or simple stone
here almost from the origin
resume my time

If death has not room
I will find
a quiet star without a moon
to keep me up
on summer nights
longing heated
dreamless as
the mind which masters visions
and exchanges images for space
and replaces time with breathlessness

July 7, 2000

Wrensong

Awakening to wrensong,
is as if my thoughts were sung
by the surrounding air

Lying down to sleep,
I hear the few birds that are up
discuss the day melodically

A sky opens with rain and
pirouettes all that has been,
a choreography of memory

honoring everyone,
and the woodchuck and the rabbit
and the deer

July 8, 1998

A Glorious Summer's Day

A Glorious summer's day.
Do the dead dwell within the flowering?
Soul of veronica, yarrow, and lady's mantle.
Relinquishing form,
do they survive on scent and color?

The dead wait easily for blooms —
swathes of annuals,
biennials,
transplanted peonies.
Their patience is infinite
and awakens true formlessness.

In cool, reflective darkness,
away from the overbright sun,
the wilderness of berries
and the sturdiness of shrubs.
I remember who I thought my parents were,
who they are now,
and that we fall to nothing,
save each day's stillness or breeze.

July 11, 1993

Neighborhood Picnic

From fading roses, snappeas, and lettuce
I learn
harvest has an exact moment

The neighborhood picnic has changed
 character, again,
overrun by children and young couples,
my parents tell me

That same damn deer
parades the lawn
shamelessly,
having eaten Mother's lilies and pansies
during the night

And the forty-first woodchuck,
lured by a carrot,
released in distant woods
whimpered telepathically:
I   have a mate

So Dad sets the traps again
We eat the first zucchini
Words sweep the cooling trees
snatched by the pool frog
along with spider supper
Perhaps he will swallow them once and for all
bestowing blessing upon blessing

July 15, 1996

Summering

The trees are still here
leaning over the drive
like friendly conspirators

the eyes can rest
and the mind

It takes a day
sometimes a night
to refill
the reservoir of the heart
to wait
for the story to stop

to be engulfed
Japanese red maple
blue salvia

Mists convene the aortas of being
Will they stop the gaps
Will it be they who tell me
when I am made final

perfectly prepared to pull a weed
or harvest a cabbage with compassion
in my mad garden

July 16, 2001

Woodchuck

The woodchuck and I come to the end of a
     morning together,
he in his hole near the vegetable garden.

Nature hurries through summer.
I continue to hold the blooms in mind,
remembering Mother.
The animals and birds seem our inheritors,
hers and mine.
I discover a seed, a nut, on a doorsill,
probably left by a squirrel,
and take it as a symbol:
think of the future, not the past,
or, at least, let go...

On a branch nearby and up above,
nesting in a gourd,
the wren's new brood.

July 26, 1996

Air Tragedy

That flash of recognition
among early evening stars
the flash that tinges everything

In one moment
Time becomes a miracle
that is over
finished
a flattened wave
And those final seconds
pound against you
like a lover
you thought you would never see again

July 1993

Picking Peas on Earth

For Mom and Dad

Rattle your seedcases
my peas
clamoring to be eaten

I brave untimely heat
slugs   bees   scratchy borage
mosquito forays

You rattle at buzzing coneflowers
I am reminded of
Sousa in a shell
Aphrodite in dotted swiss
alone in my skin
rattling bones
rattat rattat rattat

Flesh disappears
devoured by flailing music
The Great Tambor
releases tangerine light
Dream escape foiled by tomatoes
waiting to be tied to stakes
like witches

And I desire to weep for its own sake
like Mother
wishing to change nothing
The Great Prayer Wheel spins
and whirls and winds down
into what is supposed to be
some sort of ending —
sleep perhaps
a jig
a fling
even a soulful rendering
as when the backyard cardinal
improvises an auld lang syne
one more time

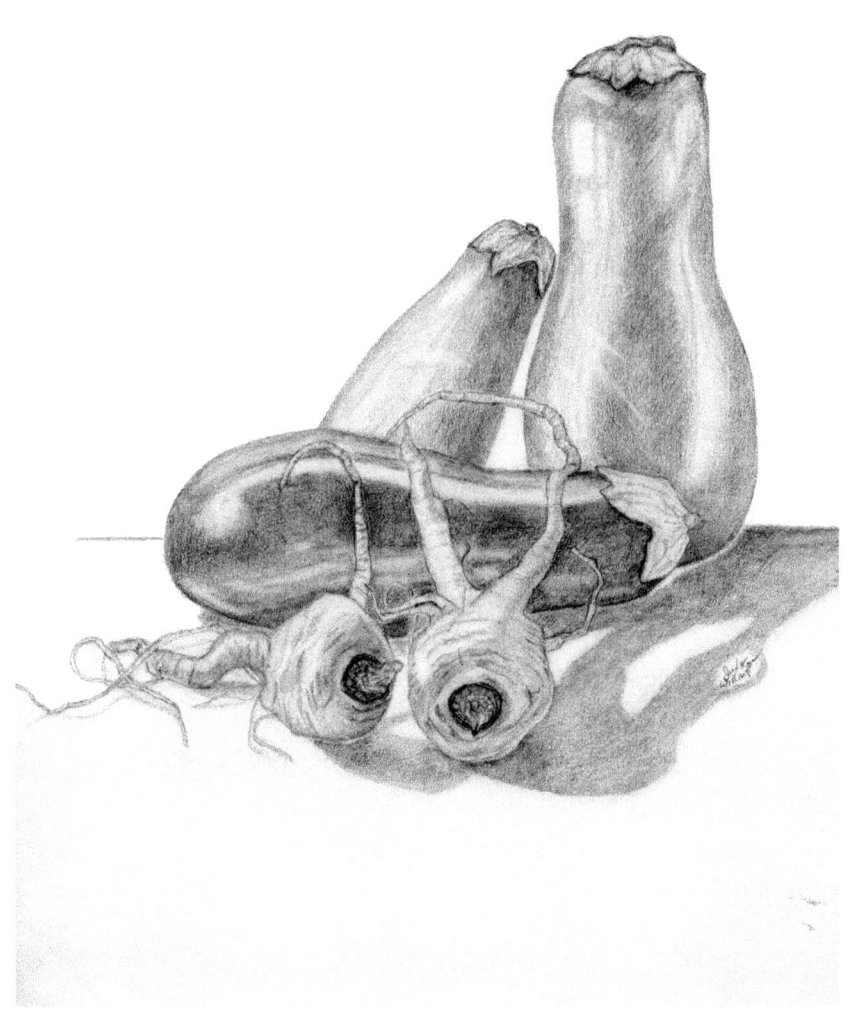

July 2002

In the Garden

Late afternoons and evenings fill the air with smoke
from fires burning in Quebec,
testing our resistance to this hot and humid weather.

Pruning, weeding, watering,
our work is an incentive to keep going
through the brief extent of time
we both know I have left.

We tent the blueberries.
The catbird watches us.
Leftover lengths of rowcovers,
sewed and pinned, billow up
around the skyward reaching branches.

Later, when we walk back up the slope
to doublecheck,
we find the bird entangled in our makeshift net.
We give him time and wait for his escape.
Once free, he perches on a garden fence
and calls across the property.

We left the berries to the birds last summer.
This year, we make a valiant effort,
aware our hearts have little faith in it.

We try to hide the fruit from view
yet quietly renounce the harvest.

As they are captured or fall to earth,
the blueberries seem a last request.

August 7, 1994

Waking in Paradise

The sun rises

I wait, as if in expectation
of an ancient rite

Sweeps of perfection arise —
cleome, cosmos, zinnia —
comforting, evocative blooms
in looseknit order

Some open too quickly,
no appetite for waiting,
wanting all to be over

I listen to dawn,
to mist above blue water,
lit treetops midsummer full

The sun starts coming up behind me
like the neighbor's cat
Stalking prey he then will swallow,
he bites off the head
and later offers up the fur and bones

August 17, 1998

Monday Morning, August

A fine rain won't break the flowers,
this Monday morning.

The catbird trills,
the clock chimes,
and wrens warble,
proverbial and therapeutic.
Listening is a feat of forgiveness.

The season brings time around
to where it needs to be.
O single Zinnia gracing the kitchen table!
Your stem supports a shade-of-pink blossom,
the sound of rain,
and birds,
and your presence,
whose color I cannot describe.

August 2002

An Old Maple

The tree has always seemed to us
a rootedness in years and lives,
branching wide across a spread of moss.

This is where our parents lived and died.
And I now claim it as my own,
the right location for my death.
Over the years, the woods have grown so tall,
the once strong winds that filled the afternoon
diminish to a gentle breeze.

This air is rooted here.
The treetops, tangled in it, speak,
and have since when the house and lawn
were carved out of the property.
They resonate to what has been alive,
what may continue, what may not.

Whoever comes to work, to dig or plant,
to prune or mow, becomes a fixture
of the landscape, too.
In future, some sage, painter-owner will
detail the tree, the woods, and all.
Meanwhile, I wait my turn beside
the aging maple and the sunburnt lawn.

Undated

Gladioli, Equinox '99

white gladioli, red-streaked,
where you planted them,
had not shown
when you died
in mid-september

the summer following,
blood-streaked gladioli
absorbed my eyes,
my desire to follow you ran wild

this time, another september,
only leaves remain,
aching, flowerfree
among the living blooms

September 23, 1997

Elegy to Mother and Dad

The cold air blew in after burial.
As you predicted, Mother,
it will be an early fall.

I return to the hill,
that afternoon in the cemetery
of finished poplar and pine.
I return to the mourners at our backs,
like a bristling ritual of wind.

September 1990

Mid-day

You arrive as morning peaks

I know You, Reflection of woods
in the windowglass
Treefrogs call to listen
Dryer, tumbling laundered towels

I spend hours with books on perennials and
herbs,
clip dead phlox and Meidiland roses

Tomato incense chokes the air as
September ruffles fern and fir

You and I, we hover near the equinox,
a seam of time
and butterflies interpret flowers

September 1994

Growing Seasons

Tomatoes grow everywhere,
make up for last year's small crop
In mid September,
the final few ripen
A lovely cool day follows
a chilly night

I hear the howl of winter
and my name is spoken
somewhere inside that sound

A name—
like a crow weighing down
a branch of tree,
deer feasting on our hearts,
tomatoes crystallized into summer's rubies
set in circlets of dying vines

Undated

Fifth Anniversary

The sound of the breeze from the fan
The sound in the brick
Mother wakes me near her birthday,
this year,
the fifth anniversary of her death

Early 1990s

End of September

Mother, why suffer so
as morning enters afternoon,
as everything dies
and is not yet reborn

Mother, I have picked your late Garden
bare
except for a wilt of herbs
and flowers

You,
at this deep Transience of year,
have picked me dry

although the rainfall barely stops
have picked me dry
and left my bones

You persevere
The weakened bee riding
paling flower
cannot let go that late sweet heart

a final pepper reddening
near the Woods
Exquisitely Alone

expresses what it is like to grow
imperceptible slow and silent
as if the Universe were
Your empty relic of summer

August 1990

Country Room

Nature has extended our parents' house into her own
    region.
She has made an example of them,
aging people who live as many live,
eating improperly and watching too much television.
Nature understands retirement.
She sees the unseen because it is She
and Four Frogs who preside over the pool
and Three Purple Grackles
who range the lawn for grubs each morning.

Mother's perennials are beautiful
but she planted too many tomatoes
and yellow squash and not enough else.
Next year, she says, no vegetable garden.
Next year, if I am here, she says.
She guides me through papers and china,
boxes and trunks in the cellar,
and wants to be buried in her pink dress.

Decorated by Mother, my country room
is yellow like my childhood rooms
of men who sell balloons; giraffes and flowers.
I cannot remember when I told her
yellow was my favorite color.

July 1989

What's Wrong with Dying

Nature is deaf to their shouts —
absorbed by green
swept away by wind
vibrating off bark and stone

They say the first owner's wife died here
She loved the house her husband built
of wooden ships he sailed —
the porthole next to the front door
the bunk in the den
the figurehead over the fireplace

Why shouldn't she die in the house she loved
Mother wants to die here too
where she sculpted and planted her gardens
where we had the awful argument

House on a windy hill
Trees tall enough to frighten and beautify
Swimming pool like a call to purity

Although the male may write the will,
the deed of inheritance,
what woman prizes is from her mother

October 1990

Suburban Elegy

This is it
the end of summer

Geese are overheard
even in the city

Blooms of memory shine:
tall white snapdragons
in slanted light,
Mother's marigolds—
the season's strip of survivors—
although marigolds make us sneeze

If anyone told me
we'd be friends,
Mother and I,
I would have shrieked with laughter
or wept

She works through dinnertime
in her perennial garden

When you're gone, I tell her,
I'll place your favorite flowers
here on the kitchen table

Bend a head or stem
so I'll know you're near

Even Houdini couldn't do it,
says Mother

You can, you will, you have to,
I think you must do it, Mother,
for the sake of the years
we didn't know we loved each other

If I go first, Mother,
make it daffodils
or whatever's in season

October 1997

In Memory of Mom and Dad

Death is always sudden.
The iced-up hemlock,
split to its trunk.

Last year's storm and this
coalesce.
Trees crash all night
in the north woods,
near where the dog sunned
each morning.

Mother,
I hear your bathwater running.
Dad, asleep,
head dropped to his chest,
breathes in tv.

I grieve, as with each fall of treetrunk or vine,
chainsaw echoes from thicket to lawn
to within my darkened grove of bones.

October 10, 2000

Unmaking the Bed

After death you strip the bed,
each pillowcase and sheet
left in a heap

the leaves of a tree drop simultaneously
the earth on its concluding spin toward finality
a tear that cannot disappear

October 21, 1997

On Our Parents' Death

I-84, Middlebury, Connecticut
September 15, 1997

The woods wade in fallen leaves.
Mother continues to believe herself real,
while zinnias fade across her breasts.

Oh, she is the lucky one.
We, left homeless in her home
watering white mums
that grow fuzzy as the winter when it comes.

The blood on the handbag
may not be her own.
Daily I say, "I will throw the pocketbook away."

Dad's ghost filled the den
until we poured his ashes on the ocean.
Someone said, "Touch them."
Our fingertips, lit, still burn.

Mom's spirit rides the garden gate with
    wild abandon,
calling: "Husband! Why did we leave
our daughters whom I loved
like blue salvia and the calla lily?"

October 1999

An Epitaph for Ashes

For Andy

Deer browse and chase one another
through woods and across lawns,
like breeze or children playing

I am reminded
of the Buddha's parklike home
where he grew restless,
kept from knowing the world around him

Once outside
he grasped at understanding

One imagines a vivid autumn morning,
leaves like brightly-colored flags
The leaves plummet to earth,
and as they do, they murmur and rustle
of an end to suffering

Undated

Harvest 1996

Wrapped in the arms of Autumn
which I pray will protect me
from its own rash winds,
I scavenge the garden.

Summer hay is scattered
like the memories
I am lost in.

My thoughts bow among
wavering locust trees
which tower above their brethren.
Near the crest of the hill,
a family of deer file
securely within
what will be winter's skin.

O renunciate Autumn,
sacrifice your heart,
leaves circulating endlessly
in the Body of Wind.
Sunflower faces droop,
crumbling at a chicadee's whim.

I release the past
in exhaled breath

and inhale Seasonal Belief
in stalks of brussel sprouts
savoring first frost,
buried beets, with blooms
of reddened, cold-burned leaves,
a bed of salad greens in wild array
sacred as a trysting place.

October 2000

Cadence

For Javier

These leaves fall quickly,
those seem to wait.
Assemblies of them fill the tops of trees.

This gray autumn day,
the lyric wakes
outside our windows primed for storms.
Gusts shift our thoughts toward what has come
before.

There is nothing to stop memory.
It circles like the wind between evergreens,
lifting boughs,
between branches of the deciduous trees,
raining leaves.

And gathering.
The mounds and streams of what whirls sculpt
new contours for the reticent earth you love.
The way that you love me,
and one day I will love.

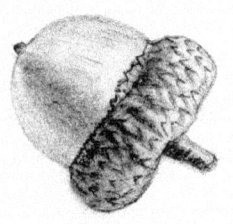 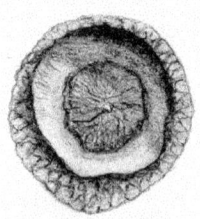

November 17, 1999

Acorns

The squirrel prays against my death
He bargains with acorns,
his small, sharp claws scooping holes
under the dogwood tree

or he petitions
statuelike
on hind legs
in profile

He is my charm
for my own not praying

From the woods, an odor of decay
Perhaps a deer a coyote got

I am told
but cannot catch the reek of it,
nostrils shut to the scent
of what is alien

At this moment
death is alien
although I am told
it holds the nut of love within its grasp

Undated

Nearwinter Sun Is Rising

Nearwinter sun is rising on a hill
beyond a house
where locusts lean
and share a sense
of how space ought to feel
    The sun, a golden apple
    tossed as if by dream

November 1993

Each Shape

Meanings fail
beautifully
Rhythms form, unform

A buck in motion—
concentrated bursts like quick thought
set aside on second thought—
returns his camouflage
to woodland

Overhead
clearspeaking clouds
with chill November breath
practice patterning the space
that lawn allows the sky

The squirrel flicks its tail
and leaps
into the privacy of the brush
as a crow calls to land

We uncover a cache:
the perfect body of the day

December 9, 2001

Exceptions

Death makes no exceptions
The Japanese red maple is gone
after too many dry years
its leaves curled like dead fingers
They remain on the tree
a reminder of what has happened here

December 1994

After Thanksgiving

This time of year makes love
to the nakedness of weathered trees
Darkened deer graze among heaps
of yellowed leaves,
white tails interrogative

This time of year I died
once and will again—
early December, late year,
a shrift of space

The deer and I grace
summer's remaining blades
The near tall trees branched
like antennae
or antlers
against a fallow sky
Leave us this peace
protect
sense everything for us

December 1993

Winter Arrives

Winter arrives
robed in natural mourning:
frozen heavens
stiff-branched maple
empty beds

The colorless landscape craves hue
and we wonder what passions to renew
as the cold comes in

A squirrel loses its footing
on the feeder
and waits for birds
to spill nourishment
out onto the grass

Answers arrive
in small doses,
a supplement
each time the feeder
is filled

December early 1990s

The Paperweight

for my father

There it sits,
like the heart of the house.
Underneath,
the bills and calculations of a life.

A tv and a telephone.
Bronzed babyshoes on marble.
A stopped clock.

The heaviness of evening,
like the dog's snoring to cricket rhythms.
The wooden room of batteries, how to's, pencils.

There is no one here.
No one calls and no one answers.
The dog snores and papers pile up.
The mail's getting old.
Soon the weight won't hold.

December 23, 2000

Arcadian Gardens

We sat out on the patio.
White flowers glazed a summer's night.

In winter, under a cold aegis of sun,
trails made by voles on the snowfield crisscross one
      another
like the paths of tipsy skiers.
Squirrels, urgent, hunt what they have hidden away,
leaving potholes in the snow.

We squirrel ourselves into the depths of the house
and seal things up tight as a drum,
although not enough to prevent the chill
from entering us.

A weak sun dissolves the snow off the boughs of
      hemlocks.
Mother's shriek when the car hit strikes my heart,
      again.
But now it too has weakened,
as if what was frozen simply melted to water and was
      never ripped
from trees, from life, by the winds of life,
was never hurled to earth.

December 1997

Poem to Death, Winter Solstice

I am like a beautiful song
you cannot help singing.
As you observe cold snow beneath
the moon,
my lips caress your heart,
your treelimb shadows.
Yet, you are unhappy, thinking:
she is neither old
nor ready for her pain.

I ask you to be joyful on your arrival.
Seem to see my spirit dreaming,
kin to the melt of iced-up gardens,
eternity expressing its perfection
as uncertainty

Reflections on *Elegy*

From Vivian Shipley

Meditations crafted by an emotionally complex mind, poems in *Elegy* are as deeply felt as a prayer. "Vibrant with the state of not waiting," emphasizing the importance of savoring life that is present, Raphaela Willington faces not only the death of her mother and father but her own certain death from ovarian cancer. Believing that the perfection of eternity is learning to live with uncertainty, Willington transforms into a mourning dove winging onto a branch "that may or may not hold me." In order to shut out despair that is a constant companion, she plants paperwhites that become a sacrament, hangs birdhouse gourds and watches a cardinal that is a "perfect foil" for winter. In her vision, gold forsythia and cherry blossoms become jewels.

Rather than focusing on how few days may be left, she counts the number of woodchucks—forty-one—that she has helped to catch and release. By creating poems that freeze a particular event, she brings us moments of celebration. The gravity of death weights these poems, but there is always light in the shadow and ultimately Willington gives us a message of hope by showing how the human spirit can struggles with the blackness and uncertainty of death and not be broken.

Poems teach us to use our eyes, our ears to bind us to others in a world that threatens to drown out the cry for life in the midst of the din. What unites this intense and compelling collection is the Willington's knowledge that the heart must find a voice in order to ferry us from life to death.

Vivian Shipley's eighth book of poetry, All of Your Messages Have Been Erased *(Southeastern Louisiana University Press, 2010), was nominated for the Pulitzer Prize. She won the 2011 Sheila Motton Prize from the New England Poetry Club, the Paterson Prize for Sustained Literary Achievement, and the Connecticut Press Club Book Prize for Creative Work.*

From Theresa Senato Edwards

Raphaela Willington's *Elegy* gracefully glides through a decade of recollection, yet purposefully modulates from one year to another, giving us **the poet's** sense of that uncertain longing found in all natural landscapes, whether seasons, creatures, mother, father, self. And with her inventive use of personification, we are able to experience when the squirrel "brilliantly bargains" against death or when "answers arrive / in small doses." We are also given the truth of mortality, when a "maggot-ridden, halved, / and disemboweled" squirrel helps the speaker find her "other self ... waiting to be joined / to earth." Although the title is fitting for Willington's lament, the overtones in this collection do not just emit sorrow or the circling of memory "between evergreens"; they also impart starkness, simplicity, and surrender to "a beautiful song / you cannot help singing."

Theresa Senato Edwards is author of Voices Through Skin *and* Painting Czeslawa Kwoka ~ Honoring Children of the Holocaust.

From Elizabeth Cohen

After her parents were killed in a freak accident and she became sick with ovarian cancer, Raphaela Willington became very quickly, and intimately acquainted with death. Rather than sink into self pity or despair, she decided to probe and parse it, and get to know it, its wiles and ways, the ways it effects us and all things in the natural world. In the end, she found in death a muse. Like those people who return from near death experiences to describe a white light, Rapheala shows us the many shapes and colors of death, she studies its demeanor, she examines it clothed and naked—from the "homelessness" of bones, to a disemboweled "mangled squirrel."

In her poems, so beautifully collected and edited by her lifelong friend John Briggs, she has done the near impossible, gotten up close to the end of life and found the beauty there. In Elegy, Raphaela is death's anthropologist. These are so much more than poems. They are excavations, prayers, obituaries; they are whispers and magic incantations from that place we dare not look. Rapheala looks for us, and what she finds in the terrible is the beauty in decay, the "pungent, white" gorgeous stories, its truths.

Elizabeth Cohen's books include The Family on Beartown

Road: A Memoir of Learning and Forgetting *(Random House, 2003)*, The Scalpel and the Silver Bear *(Bantam Books, 1998)*, Impossible Furniture *(Nightshade Press, 1993)*, and The Hypothetical Girl *(forthcoming)*.

From James R. Scrimgeour

Raphaela Willington's poems illustrate an existential truth: the act of facing death squarely and honestly adds an important dimension to human life. There is "no fitter ending" for her bones, she tells us, "than lying strewn upon the ground like willow fronds," but in these poems, the bones and/or the "mangled squirrel" are not the total being. In these poems, we see as well the "other self," the self that "honors everyone, and the woodchucks and the rabbit and the deer." As Raphaela faces squarely the real crows, she becomes free to write these poems; the "inner crows" become free to "illuminate our minds with acts of deathless love."

James R. Scrimgeour is the author of The Route and Other Poems, Monet in the Twentieth Century *and seven other collections of poetry.*

From Eric Lewis, "Wrensong," a Song Cycle

Violinist and composer Eric Lewis has fashioned poems from Raphaela Willington's *Elegy* into a song cycle entitled "Wrensong." Lewis's cycle premiered Oct. 15, 2012, at Ives Concert Hall, Western Connecticut State University in Danbury during the week of the visit to His Holiness The 14th Dalai Lama to WCSU.

"Willington's life story is very spiritually charged," Lewis told writer Rober Taylor. "When she wrote these poems, she was suffering in many ways. I could hear very clearly the music in her words: life in nature, memories of her parents, her own dreams, and the revelations of her Buddhist faith."

Lewis's cycle progresses through six songs inspired by Willington's experience of the natural world, her spiritual reflections, and her observations on the human condition. The cycle begins with "Epitaph for Ashes," and continues through "Like an Animal," "Sometimes You Wake" and the cycle's title piece, "Wrensong." Lewis observed that his musical score seeks to capture the varied themes of the poetry, from the reflective call to compassion of "Epitaph" to the rich instrumental tone of "Animal" and the progression from dreamlike state to consciousness in "Sometimes You Wake." Sounds of the natural world figure prominently in the song cycle, as in music recalling the singing of wrens each morning in their flower box nest outside Willington's window.

"'Wrensong' emerges from sleep and has bird song enter our thoughts, discussing the day," Lewis said. "It's really about birds from their point of view, communicating with each other."

The fifth song in the cycle, "Memory," draws its inspiration from a poem that seeks remembrance and order amid a cacophony of thoughts, reflected in dissonant but colorful clusters of chords and use of the soprano timber in humming that blends with the instrumental music. The cycle concludes with "The Revelation," a song in which the poet faces her own mortality and discovers new revelations about her life and her world.

The conclusion holds special resonance for Lewis, who suffered a heart attack early in 2012 that brought him to reevaluate his artistic work and take new directions.

"You instantly become mortal — and that's quite a good thing," he recalled of his illness. "It spurred me to action, to rediscover my persona as a composer, which I had put aside for so many years. When you have faced your mortality, things always become richer — the colors are much more vivid, every vibration of music has a significance it didn't have before. I understand so much better the wonderful connection between poetry and music."

OTHER TITLES PUBLISHED BY UNBOUND CONTENT

The Pomegranate Papers
by Cassie Premo Steele

Saltian
by Alice Shapiro

A Strange Frenzy
by Dom Gabrielli

Painting Czeslawa Kwoka—Honoring Children of the Holocaust
by Theresa Senato Edwards and Lori Schreiner

A Bank Robber's Bad Luck With His Ex-Girlfriend
by KJ Hannah Greenberg

Before the Great Troubling
by Corey Mesler

In New Jersey
by Julie Ellinger Hunt

Inspiration 2 Smile
by Nate Spears

and many more.

Browse the bookshelf at
http://www.unboundcontent.com

www.ingramcontent.com/pod-product-compliance
Lightning Source LLC
Chambersburg PA
CBHW021018090426
42738CB00007B/813